Slater

NATURE CLUB

BIRDS

PETER GILL

Illustrated by
ANGELA HARGREAVES
and ISABEL BOWRING

EAGLE
BOOKS

Published by Eagle Books Limited
Vigilant House
120 Wilton Road
London SW1V 1JZ
England

Copyright © 1990 Eagle Books Limited

A CIP catalogue record for this book is
available from the British Library.

ISBN: 1-85511-016-4

Designed by COOPER · WILSON, London
Design consultant James Marks
Printed in the U.S.A.

Nature Club Notes

You only need simple equipment to enjoy watching birds — a field guide, binoculars, suitable clothes, and a field notebook will do.

A diary is useful for writing up your field notes. By keeping such a diary, you will be able to record when migrating birds depart and arrive. If you also note the weather when you spot certain birds you can check if this has anything to do with their comings and goings.

If the numbers of a particular bird increase or decline, you can try to figure out the reasons for these changes.

Consider the birds' welfare when you watch them. A hungry, tired, migrating bird may be seeking the food it needs to stay alive, so do not disturb it. If you frighten a mother bird away from her nest, she may not return. Without her warmth, none of the eggs will hatch.

Wear dull-coloured clothes. The less you are noticed, the more you will see. Move quietly. Better still, don't move at all. Find a place, preferably hidden by bushes or long grass, and sit there. By going to look for birds, you alert them to your presence. You will be surprised how many birds will come close to you if they don't know you are there.

You can attract many birds to your garden by providing food. Give them nuts, or scatter seeds on the ground, or preferably on a bird table, if you have one. When putting food on the ground, be sure it is away from bushes that could hide a stalking cat.

If you provide nestboxes in safe places, they will soon be used. When puddles are frozen, some fresh water will help birds survive a cold spell. Always put the birds' welfare first.

Contents

Man's Interest in Birds

Hold a feather in your hand and feel how light it is. Unlike our bodies, birds' bodies are designed for flying. Their hollow bones are filled with air to keep them light. They have no teeth, since teeth are heavy. And they walk on two legs because their forelimbs developed into wings.

For centuries, man tried to imitate birds' ability to fly, without success. First, inventors attempted to glide through the air on artificial wings. When that failed, they tried to build planes. But early planes wouldn't take off, or quickly fell to the ground. The fastest bird, the white-throated spinetail swift, can fly over 160 kilometres per hour. A plane only reached this speed in 1912.

Birds have been useful to us since early times. Our ancestors probably became the first birdwatchers when they found that birds and their eggs were good to eat.

Indian warriors wore the majestic eagle's feathers as a symbol of their own powers.

White-throated Spinetail swift

Feathers have long been treasured for decoration and used to fill quilts and pillows. Chinese and Japanese fishermen use cormorants to catch fish, first slipping a ring around the bird's neck to stop it from swallowing the fish.

Homing pigeons have faithfully delivered messages in war and emergencies. Racing them remains a popular sport.

Birds work for us in other ways, too. Without birds of prey, such as owls, to keep down their numbers, we would be overrun by millions of mice and rats. They also kill rabbits and voles that destroy farmers' crops. Harmful insects are eaten by a vast variety of birds. Gulls and other scavengers help to clean up our rubbish.

Down from eider ducks still makes the warmest quilts.

Falconry, using falcons or other birds of prey for hunting, was a favourite sport in the Middle Ages. The best falcons were reserved for kings and princes. Noblemen and ladies had to make do with second best.

Habitat

Each species of bird has evolved to make the most of a particular *habitat* – the place where it lives – by feeding on the plants or animals there and finding a good place to nest. You may have to look hard, because many birds blend into their surroundings to hide from their enemies. A field guide will tell you where to find different kinds of birds.

Some species, like rooks, nest together, while others create their own territory.

The kingfisher may control up to a mile of riverbank, chasing other kingfishers away.

In a marshy area, you can expect to see many small birds feeding on the plentiful insects that hatch in the reeds.

Hobby

Sedge warbler

Nightjar

Crested tit

Bearded tit

Chiffchaff

Other birds probe in the mud to find
worms and grubs. A hawk may flash by,
hoping to catch an unwary bird.

In woodlands, some birds like to feed and nest in
conifers. Others prefer broadleaved trees. Some
seek their food in the treetops, while others
search among the shrubs and plants of
the woodland floor. Trees may contain
nests at the fork or the end of a branch,
or in holes in their trunks, which may
have been made by woodpeckers.

Birds you see away from their usual
habitat may be feeding and resting on
their long migration journey. Stay very
still, as the slightest movement can scare
them away.

Behaviour

When you observe birds, look closely at how they behave. Do they walk or hop? Do they climb up or down a tree? Note their flight pattern, or listen to their song and alarm calls. These, along with their colour, shape and size, are clues that will help you identify what you have seen.

A small brown bird creeping up a tree-trunk, seeking insects in the bark, can only be a tree-creeper.

Starlings swarm in vast flocks in cities and the countryside. Just by weight of their numbers they can break the branch off a tree! Their noisy clamour is unmistakable.

Tree-creeper

In feeding flocks, watch for different behaviour. Dunlins probe rapidly into the mud. Oystercatchers find and open cockles and mussels. Turnstones lift stones and seaweed to find insects.

Oystercatcher

Skylark

Some birds sing from a post or high branch, or even in flight. Others are difficult to see as they sing deep among reeds or bushes.

Waders, like the oystercatcher, find safety in numbers. Following the ebb and flow of the tide on the seashore, they advance to seek their food as the wet sand is uncovered, retreating again as the waves roll in.

In Spring, most birds leave their flocks to live in pairs. They will rear a family, which stays together until the young are able to fend for themselves. This may take only days or weeks after leaving the nest. Some birds have fancy courtship rituals, in which they can display special bright feathers. Often the male feeds the female or offers her bits of nest material. The singing of a male bird to attract his partner can help you identify him.

Bullfinch

Turnstone

Dunlin

9

Flight

Different birds fly in different ways. They all fly by flapping their wings. But they do not just flap them up and down. The downstroke is downward and forward. The upstroke is upward and backward. This gives them lift.
Note, too, how they use their tail like the flaps on an aeroplane wing.

Some move their wings very fast. Others glide or soar without effort.

Wings are designed for a purpose. The buzzard has long broad wings with feathers spreading like fingers at the tips, so it can fly easily at low speeds. Its fan tail helps it to manoeuvre. Buzzards soar on rising air currents to gain and maintain height, then use their exceptional eyesight to watch for prey below. The unsuspecting rabbit has little chance of escape when a buzzard swoops down at high speed to grab it.

Gliding birds, such as the albatross, spend most of their lives over the sea. With their long narrow wings, they use the small differences in the wind speed at various heights like a glider. They can glide all day above the waves without wasting energy.

Swan

Swans, coots, and many kinds of duck reach flying speed by paddling with their feet across the surface of the water to gain enough speed to take off.

Kestrel

Most birds take off by springing into the air, using the power of their legs to help them gain speed. Swifts live, and even sleep, in the air, only landing to lay eggs and rear young. Their legs are so small that they can only take off by dropping from their nest to gain speed.

Watch how a baby bird lands — it needs practice! Many birds land like a jumbo jet, but some, like the puffin, seem to crash-land every time!

High-speed flight, for chasing prey in the air, needs wings that are long, narrow and swept-back. At high-speed, only small control movements are needed for manoeuvring, so birds like the swift have very short tails.

Hovering flight, staying in one place in the air, is achieved in two ways. Hummingbirds beat their wings so fast they can hardly be seen as they probe for the nectar deep inside flowers. They are the only bird able to fly backward. In contrast, the kestrel, sometimes called the "wind hover", flies so slowly into the wind that it stays still over one spot.

Pheasants feed on the ground, so they spend most of the time walking or running on their strong legs. When startled, they can rocket high into the air on their short broad wings with spread feathers at the tips. Then they glide into hiding a short distance away.

Hummingbird

Pheasant

Swift

11

Shape

Different kinds of birds have a variety of different shapes, but you may not have noticed that an individual bird can change its shape dramatically. An alert thrush, particularly in warm weather, is a sleek, elegant bird. In cold weather, when it is resting, it looks like a shapeless fluffy ball as it puffs out its feathers to keep itself warm. When it is *preening*, or cleaning itself, it assumes all sorts of positions, sometimes spreading its wing feathers or fanning out its tail. You need to remember just how much the shape can change when trying to identify a "new" bird.

Even at rest, the large wings of birds that soar and glide are clearly visible. Pictures of them in flight show how small the body looks compared with the large wings.

Song thrush

preening   summer   winter

12

Rüppell's griffon vulture

Herons have long necks for catching fish. These are tucked in when they rest and in flight.

Vultures feed on carcasses, so they have bare heads and necks. If they didn't their feathers would become very dirty.

Birds that dive to catch fish and need to move quickly underwater are slim and streamlined, often with pointed beaks and heads. Their legs are placed far back on their bodies to provide maximum power as they slice through the water. But this makes it hard for them to walk on land.

Different kinds of dabbling birds, which float on the water and reach down for their food, have necks of different lengths so they can feed wherever their favourite food plant grows.

Swans have the longest necks of all dabbling birds. By upending themselves, they can reach the deepest water plants.

Tawny owl

Owls have short necks but excellent eyesight. Their eyes are at the front of their heads for hunting. They can turn their heads almost completely around to see what is behind them.

Dunnock

The spotted flycatcher and the dunnock are both small brown birds, but their perching positions are very different.

Spotted flycatcher

Puffins are plump birds with a whirring flight.

As you watch more and more birds, you will notice that many, although they are the same shape, perch in a different position or move in a different way. As you become more of an expert, this will often enable you to identify a bird immediately, even when you cannot see its colour or other small details.

Blue tit acrobatics are typical of most tits.

The coot and the moorhen are both black, but sit differently on the water. They can be recognized by the colour of their beaks.

Coot

Moorhen

Dippers are found near water. They swim with their wings open, but can also walk along the bottom of streams.

Size

The size of a bird is an important clue when you are trying to identify it. Birds can be as small as the hummingbird, which often looks like a large insect, or as large as a condor, which soars on great wings spanning 3.5 metres.

The easiest way to judge the size of a bird is to compare it with one you know well, such as a robin or a blackbird. Size is measured from the tip of the beak to the tip of the tail.

Condor

Hummingbird

Plumage

A bird's feathers are an extension of its skin; they look different at the various stages of growth. First come the *down feathers*, followed by the *juvenile feathers*, then finally the *adult plumage*. Plumage can be different in males and females.

All birds have two main types of feathers. They get their shape and identity from their outer feathers, called *flight feathers*, while the inner down feathers provide warmth. When a bird fluffs itself up in winter, it is creating a blanket of warm air between the inner and outer feathers. Some feathers make birds easy to see. Others are designed to hide the bird from its enemies.

In summer, the mallard drake without its flight feathers is harder to see.

Mallard drake in courting plumage pursuing a duck.

Brighter feathers are mostly worn by the male, in order to attract the female or scare off enemies. Ptarmigans have mottled plumage in summer to hide them on the rocky ground. In winter these feathers *moult,* and are replaced by white plumage to disguise the ptarmigan in the snow.

Most cock birds are brightly coloured to attract mates and warn off rivals. Hen birds, which have to sit still to hatch their eggs, are usually duller to avoid the keen eyes of hungry predators.

Chaffinch

Herring gull

Some immature birds change their plumage over several years before taking on adult colours and patterns.

1st winter

Before they can fly, young birds rely on camouflage to avoid danger. In fact, some look so much like the ground that you can only spot them when they move.

adult

2nd winter

Ringed plover chick

Plumage

Waders and many other birds have eye-catching white wing or tail patches that show when they fly. If one member of a flock feeding on the ground senses danger and flies off, the others see a warning flash of white and immediately take off, too.

Black-tailed godwit

Oystercatcher

Wood-pigeons feed in vast flocks in the winter.

Redshank

White wing patches are large, but they are hidden when the bird is at rest.

Greenshank

Wing and tail patches help identify each species, particularly when they are in flight.

Birds' feathers weigh more than their skeletons. A swan has more than 25,000 feathers. Without feathers, birds would be unable to fly or keep warm. Small wonder they spend so much time caring for them. This process is called preening.

The bird's flexible neck enables it to reach every part of its body, wings, and tail with its beak. But it has to scratch its head with its feet! The beak is used to repair ruffled feathers, or get rid of dirt or insects. Bathing and dust-bathing also help the bird to keep its feathers clean.

Herons, which eat slimy eels and fish, have special down patches which provide fine powder for cleaning their feathers.

Most birds have oil glands under their tails, which they rub with their beaks. Then they spread the oil over their feathers to waterproof themselves.

19

Beaks

A bird's beak does many of the things you would do with your hands. The bird uses it for catching or picking up food, building its nest, preening feathers, and even for defending itself.

Flamingos have very special beaks which work upside down, sifting tiny shrimps out of the water.

The shape and length of its beak is related to the kind of food a bird eats. The most common beak is short and pointed. But look carefully and you will see that even this shape varies. The goldfinch's finely pointed beak can pick out the smallest seeds from thistles and other plants. Yet is must be thick and strong at the base to crack the seeds. Warblers, which feed on small, soft insects, have fine, pointed beaks. Since birds don't have teeth they have to swallow their food without chewing.

Eagles and all other birds of prey have strong hooked beaks for tearing their food into pieces small enough to swallow or feed to their young.

Skimmers fly just above the water surface. The lower part of their beak cuts through the water to catch small fish.

Goldfinch

Merganser

The crossed tips of a crossbill's beak enable it to prise out the seeds from deep inside pine cones.

Black-tailed godwit

Hooked beaks are used by parrots in a different way. They use the sharp tip to tear the soft flesh from fruit and the strong inner part for cracking nuts and seeds.

Many fish-eating birds have long, straight, stabbing beaks with sharp pointed ends. Gannets and kingfishers dive into the water to catch fish, while herons wait patiently for fish to swim within reach. The merganser (a kind of duck) chases small fish under water. Its beak has "saw" edges to grip the slippery fish.

Waders find worms and tiny shellfish in mud and sand. The beak of each kind of wader is just the right length to reach the particular kind of creature it eats.

Feet

All ducks have webbed feet for paddling across the water, but diving ducks use them for swimming underwater, too. In fact, each species of bird has feet and legs ideally suited to the way it lives.

Most birds are perching birds. They have three toes at the front, and one which curves around the back of the branch for a firm grip. A tendon running down the leg and around the inside of the toes is tightened by the bird's own weight, so that even when it is asleep it grasps the branch securely.

A similar-shaped foot is needed by birds of prey, not to grip or perch, but to seize live birds and animals. They have thick strong toes and curved talons which hold the prey firmly. The osprey also has sharp scales on the underside of its toes to grip the slippery wriggling fish that it snatches from the water. Most owls have soft feathers on their legs and feet to muffle the slightest sound as they drop silently on their prey.

Osprey

The bird with the longest toes is the jacana, which is like a large moorhen. Its toes are so long that it can walk safely across floating lily leaves.

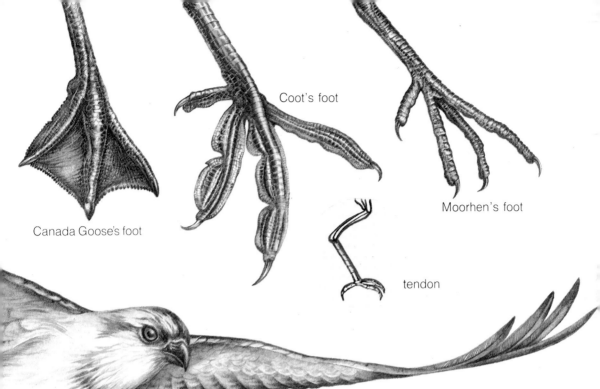

Coot's foot

Canada Goose's foot

Moorhen's foot

tendon

The ostrich has fluffy wing feathers that are useless for flying, but suit its way of life on the open plains. It has developed powerful legs with just two toes, and can run as fast as a racehorse.

While ducks have fully webbed feet to help them swim, coots and grebes have *lobes*, or rounded projections on their toes. These fold back when the foot moves forward through the water, but spread out to give a strong push on the backward power stroke.

Birds that need to move easily over soft mud or sand to find their food have long, thin, flexible toes. These spread their weight and keep them from sinking. Moorhens and many waders have this kind of foot.

23

Eggs and Nests

All birds lay eggs. The colours and shapes of their eggs are so beautiful that in the past many people collected them. Because of this, some species no longer exist, so egg collecting is now against the law.

The biggest egg is laid by the ostrich. It weighs nearly 1.8 kilograms. The smallest eggs are the hummingbird's, which lays two, each weighing little more than 2.8 milligrams. Whatever the size, the egg contains all that is necessary for the unhatched chick to develop into a grown bird. The yolk provides the nutrients, or food, for the chick's growth. Oxygen can enter through the pores in the shell, and an air sac allows the chick to breathe as it breaks free from the shell.

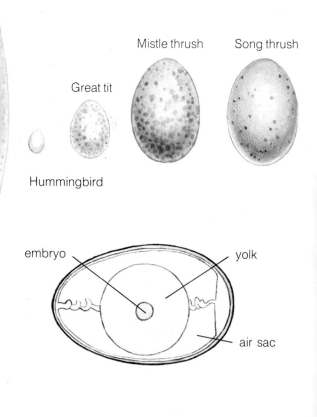

Mistle thrush

Song thrush

Great tit

Hummingbird

Ostrich

embryo

yolk

air sac

Eggs vary to suit the type of nest and the way of life of the parent birds. The ringed plover lays its eggs on pebbled ground. The eggs look so similar to the surrounding pebbles that even when you know where the nest is, it is almost impossible to find the eggs.

The single egg laid by the guillemot on a bare cliff ledge is very pointed at one end, so that it rolls in a circle instead of falling off the edge. Eggs laid in holes are usually white and round. The nest is hidden, so the eggs need no disguise, and there is little danger of them rolling away.

The tawny owl's white eggs are hidden in the nesting hole.

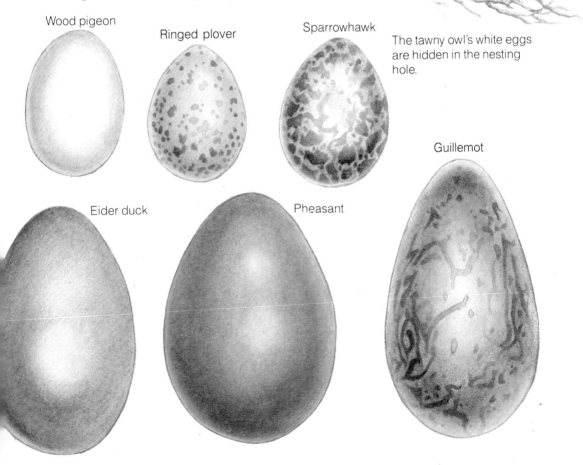

Wood pigeon

Ringed plover

Sparrowhawk

Guillemot

Eider duck

Pheasant

Eggs and Nests

Some birds return to the same nest each year. Others move from site to site. The type of nest varies according to the bird and the materials available. Some are soft and cosy, while certain penguins have to use stones because nothing else is available. Nests are normally placed to provide security from enemies and the weather.

Nests can be hard to spot. The better you know a bird's habits, the easier it is to find its nest. Droppings, such as owl pellets, are giveaway signs. If you find a nest, take only a quick look. Keeping the parent away too long might cause the eggs to chill and fail to hatch.

Eggs are never safe from predators. Magpies and weasels eat any eggs they find in a nest. Another threat is the cuckoo, which lays one egg in another bird's nest. The unsuspecting parents don't know this, because the egg looks like their own. The cuckoo hatches first and pushes the bird's own eggs out of the nest. It is then reared by its foster parents.

Some birds, like the barn owl, are now rare. As modern barns replace the old farm buildings where it nests, its home is being destroyed.

Reed Warbler's nest

One of the most complicated and beautiful nests is built by the long-tailed tit. Made of spiders' webs, moss, hair and feathers, it is often decorated with lichen. It may look delicate, but it safely holds the mother and up to twelve eggs or babies.

26

Many farmers fix nestboxes for barn owls high in new barns.

There are birds that don't make nests, but lay their eggs on the ground or in a natural hole in an old tree. Others, like the wood pigeon, make such simple twig nests that you can see the eggs from below. The swallow's nest is made only of mud. Close to the riverbank, a grebe builds a floating nest of water weeds, which rises and falls with the water level.

The most common nests are cup-shaped. Coarse grasses, roots, and fine twigs are pressed into a rounded shape by the bird's body. They are often lined with soft down and feathers, and some have a layer of mud to hold everything together.

The biggest nests are built by eagles. Each year they add new materials to it — after over 40 years one golden eagle's nest reached a depth of 14.5 metres!

Song Thrush's nest

Migration

If you watch birds regularly, you will notice that some stay around all through the year. Some disappear in winter and others arrive.

These arrivals and departures, called *migration*, have two main causes. Many birds cannot find the food they need at a particular time of year, so they fly elsewhere. Many kinds of seabirds spend most of their lives flying over the oceans, but return to land to nest and rear their young.

Migration, like so much in a bird's life, is *instinctive*. They are born with most of the knowledge necessary for survival. Many birds always fly the same route, following a coastline or choosing the shortest sea crossing. Even after a long journey, a swallow can find the previous year's nest. The most famous migrator is the Arctic tern, which travels between the Arctic and the Antarctic, a round trip of about 40,000 kilometres.

A small mass movement of birds that doesn't happen every year is called an *irruption*. Irruptions are sometimes caused by failure of the crop of seeds or berries the birds live on.

Flocks of crossbills fly hundreds of miles seeking fir cones to eat.

Swallows, which feed on insects, fly south in the autumn.

28

They also occur when a breeding season has been very successful, so too many birds have to share the same food supply.

Some birds make partial migrations in winter, keeping just ahead of the bad weather, to find the food they need.

Whooper swans.

Glossary

adult plumage   the feathers grown by the adult bird. The male bird's feathers are often brightly coloured for displaying during courtship.

air sac   an air-filled space in the end of the egg, which enables the chick to breathe while it breaks out of the shell.

down feathers   the soft feathers next to the bird's skin which provide insulation.

flight feathers   the wing and tail feathers used for flying.

habitat   the kind of surroundings which provide all a bird needs for living and breeding.

instinct   the behaviour patterns which are in-born in a bird or animal and do not have to be learned.

irruption   a long journey to new feeding areas which, unlike migration, does not happen regularly.

juvenile feathers   the feathers a young bird first grows. Usually they are dull and inconspicuous to provide camouflage.

lobes   flaps of skin on the toes of coots and grebes which open to give a strong backward push when swimming.

migration   a regular journey, usually every year, made to avoid severe weather and to find plentiful food.

moult   to shed worn-out feathers and grow new ones. All birds moult, usually once a year.

preening   the actions of a bird that smooth and clean its feathers.

yolk   the food inside the egg that nourishes the embryo while it grows into a young bird.

Index